101
Commonsense Gardening Tips

101
Commonsense Gardening Tips

Practical Advice from Master Gardeners

DEBORAH *and* **MICHAEL SWEETON**

The Lyons Press
Guilford, Connecticut
An Imprint of The Globe Pequot Press

Page design by Angie Capone

E-painting by Casey Shain

The Lyons Press is an imprint of the Globe Pequot Press.

Printed in Korea

10 9 8 7 6 5 4 3 2 1

The Library of Congress Cataloging-in-Publication Data is available on file.

This book is dedicated to Paul and Barbara King, who are responsible for our horticultural careers. Their willingness to risk all to start a greenhouse business and their dedication to excellence in customer service were truly inspiring. As they gave us greater opportunities in the business we learned what was necessary to grow quality flowers: knowledge, skill, and plenty of hard work. As we have built our business over the years we have learned the value of educating our customers. An educated customer becomes more passionate about gardening and seeks more and more answers. This book attempts to lay a solid foundation for novice and experienced gardeners alike as they venture into the wonderful world of plants.

Contents

Acknowledgments

We would like to thank a few people without whom none of this would have been possible. Peter and Kate Fiduccia have been the driving force behind our efforts to share our knowledge and love of gardening with as many people as possible. Dr. George Staby and Dr. Paul King have provided countless hours of horticulture education. Our two daughters, Stephanie and Samantha, help us every day, either in our greenhouses or by supporting all we do. They never complain. Last but not least, our partner Dave Barber has contributed not only his expertise but also his energy to making "the Common Sense Gardener" a reality. To all of you our heartfelt thanks.

Introduction

In 1975 my father decided that he wanted to start his own business after twenty-five years in the chemical and agriculture industry. He had been conducting research to develop soil additives to enhance water retention of plants. This work was the spark that ignited his passion for growing plants and the world of gardening. He asked if I would join him to help out for a couple of years while I was deciding what I wanted to do with my life. The more I worked with plants, the more I realized how wonderful it would be to make a living sharing my love and knowledge of gardening with everyone.

My husband and I have grown millions of plants since then, which have been enjoyed all over the United States. Even now, after so much time, it is still immensely satisfying to grow a beautiful plant and have someone else enjoy it. Right before we begin to sell a particular crop, be it hydrangeas at Easter, dahlias at Mother's Day, or poinsettias at Christmas, we stop and take a moment to look at what nature has given us. Every time, it takes our breath away.

For as long as we have been selling plants—to garden centers, to florists, and to regular people through our own garden store—we have been helping our customers understand what they are buying and how to be successful with their purchase. We realize how important garden-

ing and flowers can be in people's daily lives: The activity itself and what it produces help get us through times both good and bad.

Gardening is the number one hobby in the United States—and still growing (no pun intended). As it becomes more and more popular, so does the need for more gardening information, presented in a simple manner that is easy for people to understand. We get many questions every day from our customers. We've answered those most-asked questions in this book, and also provided material that most people wouldn't think to ask about, but really need to know if they are to be successful in their gardens. This book offers a foundation of gardening knowledge. Once you understand these basics, you can garden anywhere.

We hope you will enjoy reading and using this book as much as we've enjoyed putting it together!

—Deborah Sweeton, president,
Techni-Growers Greenhouses, Inc.

—Michael Sweeton, vice president,
Techni-Growers Greenhouses, Inc.

Shrubs *and* Trees

1 When you're planting a shrub or tree, the hole should be twice the diameter of the rootball but deep enough only to allow the top of the rootball to remain at ground level. In almost all cases avoid loosening the soil below this point so settling does not occur after you water in the shrub.

2 Know your soil type before planting. Most soils contain some mix of clay, sand, and silt. Too much of one component will create problems for the future health of your shrub unless modified. A rough test includes thorough mixing of 1 part of your soil with 4 parts of water in a clean glass jar. Allow the mixture to settle overnight. The larger particles (sand) will settle to the bottom first, the smallest particles (clay) will set- tle last—in the morning, you should see two different layers. If the mix is heavy in either of these two components, soil amendment is needed. Your local garden center can then help identify your soil type.

3 Before you begin to dig, it is always a good idea to locate and mark buried pipes and electrical lines. Hitting an underground electrical, gas, or sprinkler line is not a lot of fun and may end up costing you more than the shrub! If you notify your public service providers before you begin any major plantings, they should mark all lines for you.

4 Before planting any shrub or tree, conduct a Site Assessment Survey. This checklist of environmental factors specific to your yard should be available at most reputable garden centers. Such an exercise helps you assess: hours of sun your yard receives, soil type, water availability, and exposure factors such as wind, extreme heat, or frost. It can save you from wasting money and time later by making sure you plant the right shrub or tree in the proper conditions.

5 When planting a tree or shrub that has its rootball wrapped in burlap, it is essential to cut the string that holds the burlap in place. The burlap can be removed completely, but only if you won't destroy any roots that may have grown through. A better choice would be to simply peel the burlap down to right above the roots. This will ensure that the roots are able to escape the ball and penetrate your surrounding soil. (Make sure this is done only after the plant is situated in its planting hole at the proper height.) The burlap will disintegrate on its own in one season.

6 After planting a tree, it may be necessary to wrap the trunk—especially if you are worried about animals gnawing at the bark or about excessive water loss due to sunscald. Sunscald occurs when intense sunlight causes the bark cells to heat up rapidly. Once the cells are damaged, the bark easily splits open, leaving the shrub susceptible to disease.

Young trees are especially prone to sunscald. Purchase a quality tree wrap paper, a heavy-fibered, weatherproof material that will last for one or more seasons, from your local garden center. Start at the bottom of the tree and overlay the wrap by ½-inch increments. Secure the wrap with wire or string at the top and bottom. You can remove the tree wrap after one complete growing season, as this will have given the roots time to become established.

7 To test the drainage before planting a shrub, do a percolation test. Dig a 1-square-foot hole that's 18 inches deep and fill the hole with water. If the hole drains in one hour or less you have extremely well-draining, sandy soil. If it takes one to

seven hours to completely drain, then your soil drainage is average. Both these soil types would benefit from a mix of 1 part sphagnum peat moss to 2 parts of a quality, screened topsoil when planting. Use this mix to fill in around the shrub as you plant. If it takes eight hours or more for the hole to drain, you have poorly draining soil and you should consider creating a berm on the area you want to plant. A berm is essentially a raised bed of topsoil/native soil mix that raises the elevation of your planting area. Make sure the berm is higher than any remaining water in the hole. This keeps any plant roots from sitting in water.

8 When planting shrubs and trees in the fall, care should be taken to protect them from wind and lack of moisture. Wrap burlap around the shrub, not over the top of it. This will protect the shrub from wind while allowing snow or rain to provide moisture during the long winter months.

Most shrubs and trees require 1 inch of water a week during spring, summer, and early fall. If nature doesn't provide it, you must! Leaving your hose on a trickle for 20 minutes is much more effective than a torrent for a minute or two. Trickling water flows deep into the ground, causing the roots to follow. This gives you a stronger, healthier shrub.

Soil type determines how often a shrub will require watering in the years following its first season. Well-draining, rich soils should allow a shrub to root well and will require little additional watering in successive years. Marginal soils with poor water retention generally will need irrigation in successive years. In years of drought, second year watering is critical for shrub health.

11 Spreading mulch around your shrubs not only adds a nice finished look to your planting but is in fact vital for their health. There are many types of mulches available, ranging from wood chips to shredded hardwood bark in various colors and varieties. A 2- to 4-inch layer of mulch provides excellent winter protection and keeps the roots cool while aiding in water retention. Results: a happier, healthier shrub or tree.

12 To ensure that insects and critters do not spend the winter cozily under your mulch, rake the mulch 2 to 4 inches away from trunks until several hard frosts have come and gone. After that, it's okay to push the mulch back around the plant for winter protection.

In the fall, clean up fallen leaves and branches around the base of trees or shrubs. This debris can harbor disease and insects that can wreak havoc when spring approaches. An ounce of prevention is worth a pound of cure.

 Do not fertilize newly planted trees or shrubs during the first year. You run the risk of promoting too much new shoot growth rather than root development. You also may damage young root fibers if you subject them to fertilizer during this first year. Your objective is to get the shrub well established; there will be plenty of time to promote new growth in the future.

15 If the leader, or top branch tip, of a newly planted evergreen is damaged, cut it off and choose a new leader. Choose one of the side branches nearest the top and bend it upright. You may have to secure it in place with a splint and a strong but pliable wire. It may take a season or two, but over time the branch will strengthen and become the tree's new vertical leader.

16 Be careful when you prune. To maximize flowering, first learn the flowering habit of your shrub or tree. Plants that form flower buds on the current season's branches, such as Pee Gee hydrangea and rose of sharon, can be pruned in early spring. Plants that bloom on the previous season's branches, such as rhododendrons, should be pruned only after the blooming cycle to maximize future flowering. A good rule of thumb is to prune shrubs or nonfruiting trees within eight weeks after they have finished blooming. This will ensure that you are not removing any of the following season's flower buds.

When pruning a branch, make a cut beyond the branch-bark ridge, the swollen area at the branch base. It is a strong protective zone that will prevent decay from entering the tree after the cut. Not only will your tree be happy, but you will also be protecting your investment.

 Thinning is the selective removal of branches from the shrub base, which keeps the crown open. This practice maximizes light penetration, which keeps your shrub fully leafed out and healthy. The natural growth habit will be maintained while avoiding overstimulation of growth.

Perennials

What's the difference between an annual and a perennial? Annuals, such as Impatiens, complete their life cycle in one season. The seed germinates, grows quickly, and then sets seeds in the fall. Perennials, such as Rudbeckia (black-eyed Susans), are nonwoody plants that bloom for a shorter period but do so for more than one year. Some last a couple of years, while others last for many years. The plants die down to the ground in the winter, but the roots are persistent and the plant regrows the following spring.

General Characteristics, Annuals vs. Perennials

ANNUALS

- Most bloom all season (spring–frost)
- Most are prolific bloomers
- Most are uniform in appearance from plant to plant
- Most require little maintenance (water, fertilizer, and occasional deadheading)
- Little variety over the course of the season (display stays the same)
- Need to be re-planted each year/opportunity to change display yearly

PERENNIALS

- Most bloom for a limited period (a few weeks or so); sequence of bloom
- More "green" in the border from plants not in bloom
- More variety in sizes and shapes; tend to be more loose and open than annuals
- Some require more maintenance (staking, deadheading, dividing); others very little
- Display changes throughout the season; more variety and interest
- Live for a few years to many years

20 When selecting perennials in your favorite garden center, choose the plants with the fullest, nicest foliage and fewest blooms. Flowers drain energy from the plant and can decrease short-term vigor. You are planting perennials for many years of enjoyment, not for the short term. In fact, you should pull the flowers from newly planted perennials to channel the growth to the roots. This way you'll have a firm foundation for a healthier plant and more blooms for years to come.

21 When purchasing potted perennials, pop the perennial from the pot to check the roots before you head to the checkout counter. Avoid plants with heavy masses of thick brown roots. Look for ones with loose, creamy white to tan, soft tender roots. These perennials will transplant to the garden more easily since they will experience less transplant shock (damage to roots caused by inadequate water uptake).

22

Two critical factors for success with perennials are selecting the proper location in terms of sun exposure and determining the drainage characteristics. Always check your percolation

(perk) in areas that you want to plant, as you did for shrubs (see tip #7). Generally, water should drain from a 1-square-foot hole in one hour or less to be considered well-draining. Also, make sure you know the number of hours of direct sun for each location. This will allow you to match the right plant with the right conditions.

 23

Know the "Hardiness Zone" for your part of the country. All perennials have a winter temperature below which they cannot survive. So if you live in Zone 5 you can plant any perennial known to survive in that zone. For example, Columbine is Zone 5, which means it will "winter-over" in that zone and any warmer (Zone 6 to 11). Dicentra (bleeding hearts) are Zone 3-4; they will survive winter temperatures even colder than Columbine. A good garden center will know your zone, or you can find it online at http://www.usna.usda. gov/Hardzone/.

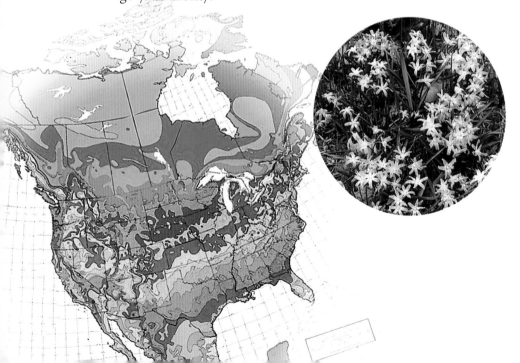

24 A new concept in gardening is the "Heat Zone" map. A plant's "Heat Zone" rating refers to how many days over 86 degrees Fahrenheit that particular plant can experience and still perform well in the garden. The country has been divided into 12 different zones. Zone 1 has an average of less than one day per year above 86 degrees. The highest zone, Zone 12, has more than 210 days per year above 86 degrees. You want to choose plants that not only winter-over in your area (see tip #23), but also tolerate the hot days in your region as well. An example would be Delphiniums. Their "Heat Zone" is 6 to 1, which means they will do well where the summer has 60 or fewer days above 86 degrees. Delphiniums may very well survive where it is hotter but their performance will be less than expected. To find the "Heat Zone" for your area go to http://www.ahs.org/garden/zipform.asp.

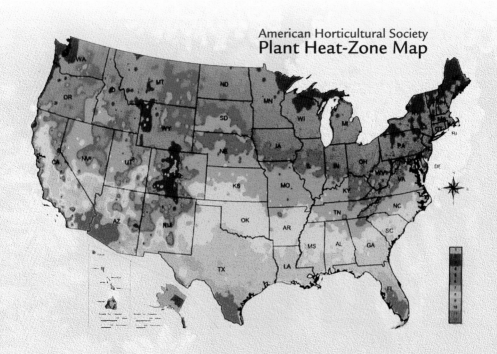

American Horticultural Society
Plant Heat-Zone Map

25 Microclimates can exist around your home and help provide safe havens for tender plants, as these areas remain warmer than exposed areas. In fact, you can successfully plant perennials that are rated for one zone warmer than the one you reside in, if you take advantage of them. Examples of microclimates include south- and west-facing sheltered locations close to your house foundation, rock walls that retain heat from the sun, and the area above your septic tank—probably the best microclimate in your yard.

26 In some hardiness zones, certain plants can be perennial but never flower. For instance, in Zone 5 or lower, hydrangeas purchased at Easter or Mother's Day would survive when planted in your yard but will never bloom again. These hydrangeas

(macrophylla) bloom on the previous year's wood (stems). This old wood does not survive the winter in Zone 5 or lower, so all you get is a nice green bush with no flowers! To avoid such disappointments, be sure to research the specific conditions for the perennial you want to plant.

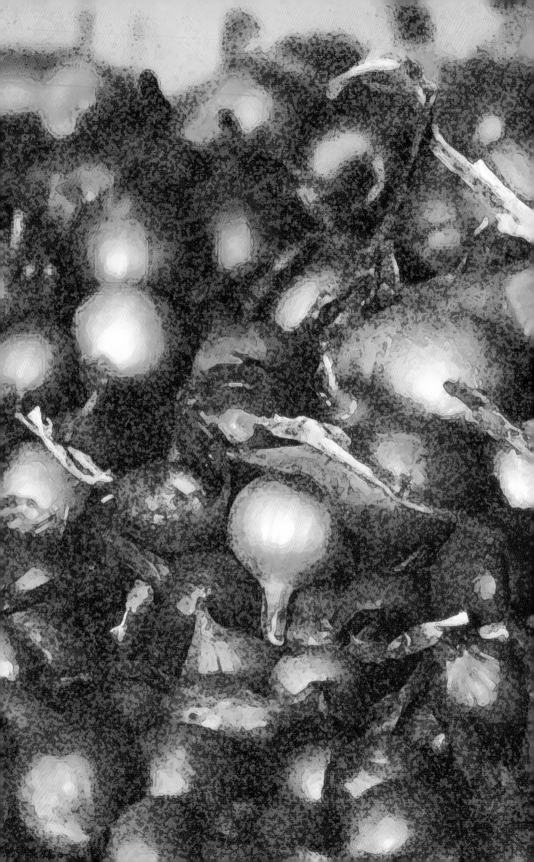

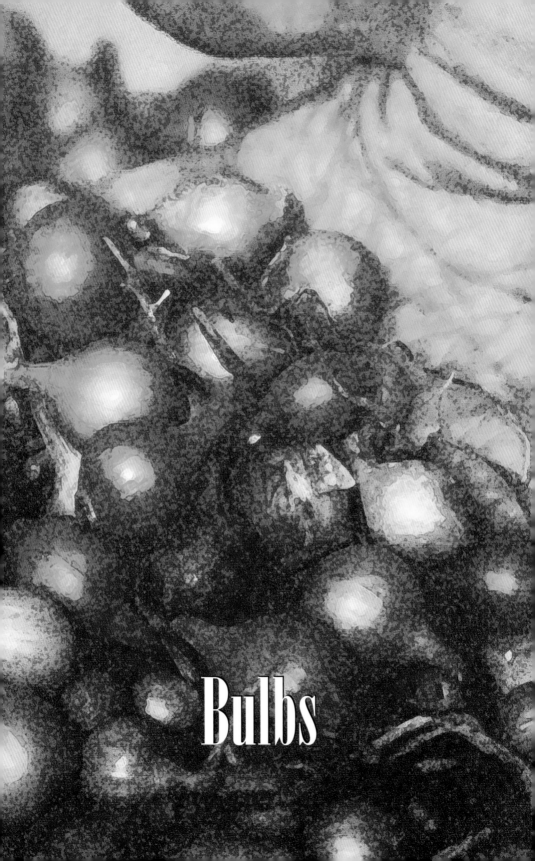

Bulbs

27 People always ask, "How deep do I plant bulbs and how many do I plant in a hole?" That depends on the size of the bulb, which is usually listed on the package. A good rule of thumb is to plant the bulb three times as deep as its length. Also, no matter how many you are planting in the hole, make it an odd number. This is more pleasing to the eye. In a 1-square-foot hole, three to seven bulbs work best.

28 Because bulbs come in many sizes with many bloom dates, it is possible to create an extended flower display in one little hole. Since most bulbs should be planted to a depth of three times their height, you can layer bulbs of different sizes. Put larger ones on the bottom, add a little soil, add smaller bulbs, and so on until you have three or four different layers. Now wait for spring and watch how long this one spot will have blooms.

29 We recommend fertilizing when you plant bulbs. Your bulbs will be healthy, produce well, and return year after year simply because you took a little time to feed them. We suggest a slow-release formula like Bulb Booster. You can use bonemeal, but the slow-release products are better because they contain extra nitrogen and potassium in addition to phosphorus. Dig your hole twice as deep as the recommended bulb planting depth— in this case, it should be six times the length of the bulb. Now sprinkle on 1 rounded teaspoon of granular slow-release bulb food per square foot.

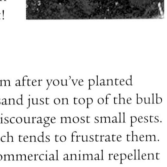

Replace half the soil removed from the hole. This will provide a good transition zone as bulb roots go deep. Place your bulbs on top (remember odd numbers) of this soil, fill in with the remaining soil, and water in thoroughly. When spring arrives, you are in for a treat!

30 Critters can sometimes be a problem after you've planted your bulbs. A 2- to 4-inch layer of sand just on top of the bulb (depending on the bulb size) will discourage most small pests. The sand collapses as they dig, which tends to frustrate them. Also, try dipping your bulbs in a commercial animal repellent before planting them. This works, but wear gloves and hold your nose. Most of these repellents have strong odors and can irritate your skin. They do discourage digging, however.

Naturalizing is a term used to describe the degree to which bulbs perennialize. Some bulb varieties such as daffodils, chionodoxa, muscari, blanda anemone, and crocus will multiply year after year and are extremely long-lived. Planted once and fertilized yearly, they will provide many years of blooming enjoyment.

If deer are a problem in your area (which is almost everywhere these days), look for bulb varieties that are deer-resistant. Daffodils and chionodoxa are proven winners when it comes to getting passed over by the local deer population. Many of the deer repellents (see tip #62) work equally well on bulbs, so on tasty varieties, especially tulips, spray away.

Roses

33 The most critical step in planting roses occurs before you head to the garden center to purchase your first plant: You need to make sure that your plot receives enough sunlight and that you have enough space to support these flowers. Roses

require a minimum of six hours of full sun per day, and should be planted away from mature trees and shrubs—at a distance of twice the diameter of the established plants—so that the roses don't have to compete for water. To minimize the risk of disease, also plan for good air circulation among your rosebushes. If you have a choice between morning sun and afternoon sun for your roses, choose morning. Morning sun will dry your rose leaves sooner, thus minimizing the risk of disease.

34 There are many classes of roses. Species, climbing, shrub, and old garden roses are all fairly hardy for the beginner. Floribundas, grandifloras, and hybrid teas are much sought after for their large flowers and long bloom periods, but these classes require a little more work for success. No matter which you choose, make sure of the source. Roses are graded from #1 (the best) to #11/2 and #2 (the lowest), so be sure of what you are paying for. The bark should be green with no blackening, and there should be no evidence of bark shriveling. The plant should have a well-developed, strong, creamy white root system with many young feeder roots.

35 The best time to prepare your new rose bed is in the fall, because this will give time for any soil amendments, such as peat moss or manure, to work prior to actual planting. Roses can grow in almost any soil, but most varieties will not tolerate poor drainage or poor aeration. If your soil is claylike, consider loosening it with a shovel down to 18 inches below the planting depth. This will break up some of the clay aggregates, creating more air spaces. If your soil is sandy, mix in ¼ part composted cow manure and ¼ part peat moss. Work in some gypsum (15 to 20 pounds per 100 square feet). Bonemeal (15 pounds per 100 square feet) will ensure enough phosphorus for good root growth in the spring.

36 Start feeding roses in early spring, four to six weeks before first blooms for plants two years old or older. For newly planted roses, wait until the first blooming cycle ends. This will ensure that you do not damage young plants before they are established. In both cases continue feeding once a month with a slow-release food until four to six weeks before the last bloom cycle. In most parts of the country this will occur in late summer (mid- to late August).

37 Roses' biggest enemies are aphids, a type of insect, as well as powdery mildew and black spot, both fungal diseases. A preventive program will best protect your roses. You can apply a granular systemic insecticide (they usually contain a plant fertilizer as well) in late spring. Once temperatures reach 85 degrees Fahrenheit and humidity starts to build, spray your roses with a fungicide every 10 to 14 days. Keep water off the foliage and remove debris from around your plants to maintain good air circulation.

38 So your roses are in full bloom and you want to take some indoors? First, find a vase and clean it with soap, water, and a 10 percent bleach solution to prevent disease. Cut each stem at a 45-degree angle using a sharp pair of pruning shears.

Make sure the stem is long enough to allow trimming later. Cut off any leaves that will be below the water level to prevent disease, but leave those above the water intact to ensure that the stem takes up water. Make a fresh 45-degree cut at the final stem length and place the stem in the vase. Fill the vase with warm water containing a good floral preservative and enjoy. Your roses should last a week or more.

39 What do you do with roses in winter? Mound up to 12 inches of soil around the rose canes. Once temperatures fall consistently below freezing, add another layer of protection such as leaves, wood chips, or pine straw. Now go inside for some hot cocoa and relax. Your roses will be fine!

Houseplants

40 Before you venture out for that new houseplant, look around your home and determine the conditions first. How much light does the room get during the day? Is the room cool or hot most of the time? Does it stay moist (for instance, a bathroom), or is it dry because of a woodstove? Spending a few minutes before your trip figuring this out will make your selection easier and more on the mark.

41 Over- or underwatering is easy to detect by checking the roots. Lift your plant out of the pot. If the roots are creamy white or ivory, then you are watering perfectly. If the roots are brown or black and fall apart when you touch them, then your plant

is definitely being overwatered. Unfortunately, once a plant has reached this point, it is probably beyond saving. How often you need to water is dependent on location (how sunny or warm), age of the plant (an old plant in a small pot), and the time of year. Generally, plants that have been in the same pot for a year or those in particularly sunny windows will need to be watered more than once per week. Plants in cool, low light rooms may only require water once per week. Always check the soil with your finger to feel how dry or moist it is. Most houseplants like to have their soil feel slightly dry before a thorough watering.

It's better to water too little than too much. Most plants can survive a few brown leaves, but few if any can survive once their roots begin to die from overwatering, which leaves the plant vulnerable to fungal disease, pests, and other pathogens. Remember, soggy roots mean big trouble!

When should you transplant? The time to transplant a house-plant is when it needs to be watered daily, or when the water hits the top of the soil and runs right through the plant out the bottom of the pot. This means your soil air space—which is where water initially resides—is now full of roots. The roots cannot absorb the water fast enough as it races by.

44   Resist the urge to move your houseplant to a new pot that is much too big. When you place a plant in a pot that is too large, you increase the chance of overwatering. You should never increase by more than one pot size. So if the plant is in a 4-inch pot (a diameter measurement), your next move should be to a 6-inch pot. Pots increase, generally, in 2-inch increments.

45   Here's a great, simple way to transplant any plant: Put an empty pot of the size your plant is in inside the new larger pot. Fill the space between the pots with a good, well-draining potting soil until it is completely full. Now carefully lift out the smaller pot and simply set your plant inside. Firm the soil around the rootball, water it, and you are done.

46 Look for clues when your plants look ill. Know the character-istics of common houseplant insects. Whiteflies swarm when you brush the leaves; spider mites cause small round yellow spots to appear on your leaf surface or, in severe cases, webs to form; mealy bugs create woolly nests at the point where a branch leaves the main stem. Aphids like new growth shoots or flower buds and will leave a sticky residue, which serves as a great host for black sooty mold growth. Knowing the signs will help you zero in on the culprit. Tip #64 will give you some ways to stop these critters in their tracks.

Nothing invigorates your houseplant more than a trip to the shower! Once a month, drag your plants to the shower and get the water flowing at room temperature. This will wash away any dust that has accumulated and flush salts that may have built up in the soil from fertilizing. Salts will burn the roots over time, so get them out. After the shower, your plants will be refreshed and renewed!

 Nothing spells trouble for houseplants more than fussing over them. We always recommend benign neglect. It's simple: Water only when the plant needs it; provide adequate light and moderate temperatures. Don't give them soggy feet, or overfertilize, especially in the winter. A summer vacation outside in the shade also works wonders. We always say, "Plants survive despite us"—and it's true.

49 Some houseplants such as pothos, philodendron, and ivies have long, trailing branches called runners. These can get quite lengthy, especially in locations with low light like offices or north-facing rooms. Don't cut these runners off. Wind them around the pot several times if necessary. Make sure you put them inside the pot in contact with the soil. The runners will root and you'll have a much fuller-looking plant. It works!

 50 Misting your houseplants is a bad idea. Constant water on the leaves creates the perfect conditions for mildew and fungal disease, and nothing ruins a plant faster than this nasty duo. If you want to create a more humid atmosphere for houseplants like ferns or orchids, a tray of pebbles is perfect. It provides dry feet for the plant, creates a reservoir for the water, and keeps the leaves dry. Set your potted plant on a bed of pebbles; as the water in the tray evaporates, it creates a more humid environment around the plant yet keeps the leaves drier.

51 Some experts recommend watering from the bottom for houseplants, especially African violets, which are particularly sensitive to cold water on their leaves. This is fine as long as you remember that the plant will absorb what water it needs in 20 minutes or less. Fill the pot's saucer with water and let the soil absorb what water it needs. Then make sure to dump any water that remains in the saucer or tray to prevent rotting the roots.

52 Houseplants need less fertilizer than most outdoor plants. If your plants begin to look light green or pale, give them a boost with a good all-purpose plant food. Liquid forms of fertilizer act faster, giving instant results, while slow-release granules work more slowly over a longer time. The benefit of using slow-release fertilizer is that you don't have to administer it as often. Don't overdo it. (For more information on fertilizers, see tip #69.)

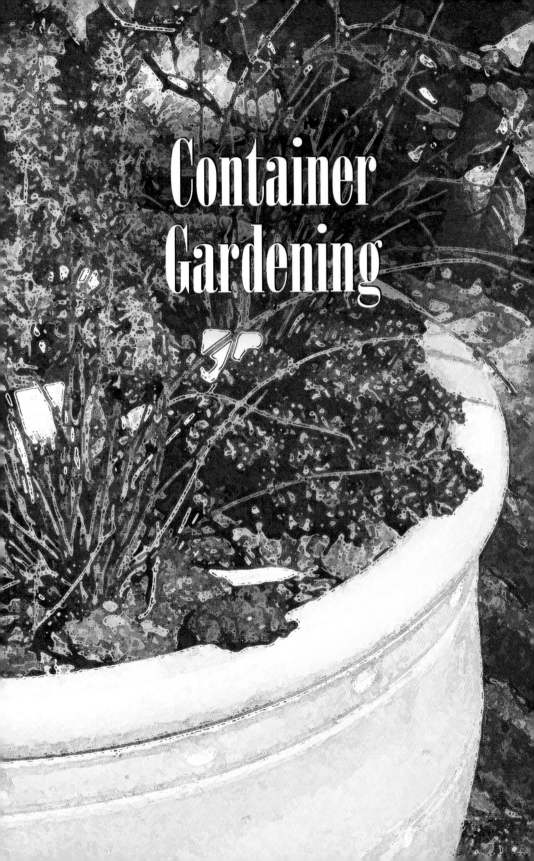

Container Gardening

53 Mixed containers or pots provide a great way for you to garden in limited-space areas like outdoor patios or porches. Designing a mixed container is easy. There are only a few basic rules. Start with a large pot size—10 inches or larger. This will give you ample space to use a nice variety of plants. Make sure all the plants require similar conditions. Use an odd number of plants; this is more pleasing to the eye. Use plants that will grow to different heights, too, as this adds interest. A mixture of tall ones in the back, shorter in the middle, and trailing plants for the edge works best. Bolder, brighter colors are more visible from a distance. Plants with white flowers or chartreuse, gray, and variegated leaves enhance the brighter colors, making them seem more vibrant.

54 When choosing plants for your combination containers, decide where the planter or baskets will be located. Figure out the number of hours of sun the location provides, how much direct wind it is subject to, and how easily water can be accessed from it. For example, you don't want to place a container of Impatiens and Lobelia in a windy location that receives sun all day, as these are shade-loving plants and both are very susceptible to wind damage. If you choose the plants that thrive in the conditions for that spot, they will live longer and your life will be easier.

55 Did you know that the labels that come with your plants are color-coded to aid you in selection? If the tag is all yellow, it means the plant needs full sun (more than six hours a day). If it's half yellow and half brown or orange, it means it needs sun or part sun (four to six hours per day). If the tag is all brown or orange, the plant is for partial to full shade (less than four hours a day of sun).

56 Annuals in containers need more fertilizer than plants in your garden bed, because the fertilizers are constantly washed out the bottom of the container. Use a combination of slow-release fertilizer and liquid food. Put in the slow-release food when you plant the container (or use a good potting soil that contains it). Use the liquid food once or twice a week, depending on the plants you have chosen.

57 Not all potting soils are created equal! Do not use topsoil or "cheap" potting soil, especially in containers. This soil is too heavy and doesn't allow adequate drainage when used in pots. Use only light, "open" mixes containing peat moss, perlite, and nutrients. They will not become waterlogged in a container. Your plants will be happier and so will you.

 58 Watering is the most important task for container gardeners. If you start out with quality plants and good soil, the only thing that can ruin your season is improper watering. As the summer progresses, your pots will dry out more quickly and will have to be watered more thoroughly as well as more often. Three things you should remember: Smaller pots dry out faster than larger ones; clay pots dry faster than plastic ones; and the older the plants get during the season, the more water they need. Also remember that rules like water only in the morning to keep the foliage dry are not cast in stone. Water your pots when they need it, as wilting is more harmful than wet leaves.

59 It's easy to make a fancy moss basket. First, soak sheet moss (available at any nursery) in a bucket of water. Line the bottom section of a wire basket with the moss and fill with a good potting soil. Gently place your small starter plants, either flowering annuals or small houseplants, in a row around the basket. Add another higher layer of moss and soil on top of these. Fill with another layer of plants but stagger them between the plants in the section just below. Continue this layering until you reach the top of the basket. Make sure you place each higher level of plants staggered from the line below. Once you reach the top of the basket, you should plant it, too. Water in thoroughly but gently so as not to wash out the soil.

When cleaning out the cellar or garage, don't throw away that old junk, plant in it! Old treasures like boots, sinks, washtubs, and wooden boxes make great planters if you remember a few things. Put a hole in it for drainage, if possible; otherwise a 2- or 3-inch layer of stone will work fine. Use a light potting mix that will allow water to drain to the stone, thus preventing root rot. In this case, make sure to choose plants that can tolerate a little stress. Have fun!

Where can you get ideas for mixed containers or simply obtain good gardening advice? We recommend a good garden center or greenhouse in your area—nothing beats developing a relationship with folks who grow plants for a living. Their displays will also give you ideas. Another great source is a good horticultural magazine. We especially like *Fine Gardening* and *Horticulture*. They contain beautiful design ideas and "botanically correct" gardening advice.

Plant Enemies *and* Nutrition

62 The number one question in late winter and early spring is "What can I use to stop the deer from eating my bulbs or shrubs?" There are many commercial sprays, but here is an easy recipe you can make at home: Blend 1 quart of water, 2 tablespoons of mineral oil, 2 tablespoons of cayenne pepper, 2 tablespoons of a liquid laundry detergent, and 1 egg. This concentrate will stay fresh for a couple of weeks in the refrigerator. Mix 1/3 cup of it with 1 quart of water, place this mix in a bottle with several holes punched in the cap, and sprinkle on your plants. Don't get the liquid in your eyes—it stings. Try applying it once and see how it goes. You will have to reapply it after a heavy rain, or if the deer keep munching, but in our experience, the deer will hate it. Get mixing!

63 Is powdery mildew a problem on your roses or African violets? If you have a white fuzzy coating on your leaf surfaces, more than likely it's mildew. One tablespoon of baking soda dissolved in 1 gallon of water plus ¼ teaspoon of dish detergent makes a great fungicide. Mix the ingredients well, put the blend in a small pump sprayer, and spray the leaves until they're completely coated. Clean up any debris around the plants, avoid water on the foliage, and reapply in 7 to 10 days if necessary.

64 A dilute solution of dish detergent and water can be a very effective cure for a minor infestation of aphids and spider mites on most houseplants (see tip #46 for insect identification). Use 1 part dish detergent to 10 parts water. Mix this thoroughly and spray it directly onto the insects. For mites, make sure you spray the undersides of the leaves until they are completely covered and the liquid runs off. Some plants can be sensitive to soap, so test it on one leaf first to see if damage occurs. You should observe any damage within a day.

65 A stream of water can also remove aphids from your plants. Place the infested leaves under a steady stream from your hose or faucet. Gently wipe the leaves or buds, removing the aphids on each section. Check your plant after the leaves dry and wash again if you see any remaining insects.

66 If mealy bugs are what's bugging you, here is the most effective method of removing the adults: Take a cotton swab dipped in rubbing alcohol and carefully swab the mealy bug crawler until it falls off. Also swab the cottony nests that tend to be wedged in where the branch leaves the main stem. Mealy bugs are persistent, so check your plant regularly before you develop a bona fide infestation.

Have you noticed small insects congregating on the soil of your potted plants? These are probably fungus gnats, a small dark-colored flying gnat. These bugs are just a nuisance, although in their larval stage they can cause root damage if the infestation is too large. Luckily they are easy to get rid of. Just let the soil in your pots dry to the touch before watering. (Be careful, however; you don't want the plants to wilt.) You should see improvement after several weeks.

 Do your houseplants look dull and dusty? A cloth or sponge dipped in whole milk and water (about half and half) makes a great leaf shine. Gently rub the cloth over the leaves; it will remove dust, grime, and water spots, leaving the leaf shiny and lustrous. Make sure you use whole milk, as the fat in the milk is what produces the shine.

 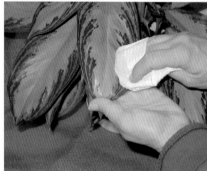

69 Slow-release fertilizer is a great invention. It comes in encapsulated pellet form, and the nutrients are released slowly over time. You typically apply this type of fertilizer only every two to three months. This saves you time and is actually better for your plants, since it makes it harder to overfertilize.

70 Choosing fertilizer doesn't need to be complicated. The three numbers on the bag (5-10-5) refer to the percentage of nitrogen, phosphorus, and potassium (N-P-K). Nitrogen promotes green leaf growth, phosphorus promotes flower production, and potassium is for strong root growth. So choose a fertilizer that meets your needs. For more flowers, choose a higher middle number or phosphorus level. For more greenery, look for a higher first number (N).

4-6-6
GUARANTEED ANALYSIS

Total Nitrogen (N) 4%
  2.8% ..... Water Soluble Nitrogen
  1.2% .... Water Insoluble Nitrogen
Available Phosphate (P$_2$O$_5$) ....
Soluble Potash (K$_2$O) 6%
Calcium (Ca) 6%
Total Magnesium (Mg) 3.0%
  0.3% ..... Water Soluble Magnesium (Mg)
Sulfur (S) ....
  5.0% .... Combined Sulfur (S)
Boron (B) ....
Chlorine (Cl) 0.02%
Cobalt (Co) 0.1%
Copper (Cu) 0.0005%
Iron (Fe) 0.05%
Total Manganese (Mn) 1.0%
  0.01% .... Water Soluble Manganese (Mn)
Molybdenum (Mo) 0.05%
Sodium (Na) 0.0005%
Zinc (Zn) 0.1%
Potent:

Watering

71 In-ground sprinkler systems can save you a lot of time if used properly. Most systems are set to turn on in the middle of the night (between midnight and 3:00 a.m.). Avoid this at all costs, since moisture and lingering humidity introduced to the turf can help in the culture or spread of many plant pathogens. Your watering should occur early enough in the morning (6:00 a.m. is a good time) that the sun can quickly dry any wet leaf surfaces.

Avoid any type of overhead watering of lawn or plants between the hours of 11:00 a.m. and 4:00 p.m. on hot, sunny summer days, since water standing on the foliage can magnify the sun and cause leaf burn. Water on the leaves also promotes fungal disease, especially on roses.

 How long is long enough when it comes to watering? Longer, less frequent applications (at least 1 inch of water twice a week) are better than daily light watering that does not penetrate the soil or reach the majority of plant root systems. You want to encourage the roots to penetrate deep into the ground, not remain shallow.

Weeding *and* Planting
Your Garden Bed

74 My mother used to say, "Weed it and reap." Monitor the garden for weeds weekly. By removing weeds before they go to flower (and then seed), you can reduce future weeding drastically.

75 Layers of 2 to 4 inches of fine organic mulch reduce weeds dramatically and keep the soil temperature cooler by helping it retain moisture.

Avoid mowing your lawn without a bag to catch the clippings. If you miss a mowing and allow it to overgrow, you will be disseminating both grass and weed seeds for introduction into the garden.

 On beautiful, sunny days an hour after you just planted that beautiful, healthy plant, does it suddenly look droopy? You haven't done anything wrong; hot sunny days simply introduce unnecessary stress to the plant's system, decreasing survival rates. Pick cool overcast days for planting. It will be easier on you, and your plants won't have that droopy, hurting look.

78 It's May 15 and it has just rained for five days. The sky is brightening and you can't wait to get out in the yard. Resist the urge. Avoid working in your garden the day after heavy periods of rain. Walking around on wet or muddy soil will cause compaction and decrease the air spaces in the soil. These air spaces are critical for healthy root growth, so don't destroy them.

79 You should almost always plant your shrubs or plants even with the ground. The exception is large plants with heavy root- or soil balls: Plant these slightly higher than ground level, allowing for the settling of the plant and soil. After a thorough watering, the plant should end up even with the ground.

80 Tomatoes are a different kind of exception. Tomato plants produce roots up the stem, so plant them deep to get a much stronger and more productive plant later in the season.

81 Avoid planting shade-loving evergreens in front of light-colored walls that may get direct winter sun. Reflection from the light surface in the winter can cause leaf damage to your plants. Rhododendrons are the most susceptible to sunscald. (See tip #6 for more on sunscald.)

Deadheading

82 Removing spent flowers of annuals and perennials in the garden before they go to seed—deadheading—will preserve plant energies, promote further blooming and increased plant vigor, and ease the need to weed unwanted garden "volunteers" in the future.

83 Many annuals need to have the spent blossoms removed, but most people are not aware that simply pulling off the flower is not enough. Make sure you take the entire flower stem and not just the petals. This sends a signal to the plant to make additional flowers rather than produce seeds. Don't send mixed messages to your flowers or you'll reap what you sow.

84 Avoid tossing your deadheaded blooms in your garden beds. They may continue to mature and go to seed, introducing a weed problem for the following season.

Fall

85 Pansies are a cool-weather crop. When planted in the fall, they will survive several light frosts, often remaining vibrant in the garden well into winter. An added surprise awaits, as these fall pansies will burst to life again in the spring.

86 Hardy mums will return reliably only if you plant them in the ground at least six weeks before a hard freeze, and make sure they get adequate water as long as they are alive. Once the frost has finally killed the foliage, cut it away and cover the plant with 4 inches of mulch. Look for emerging shoots once the ground warms in the spring. You will need to pinch these shoots as they grow. Using two fingers, pinch off the growing tip for every 2 inches of shoot length until July 4. This will ensure wonderful blooms for the next fall season.

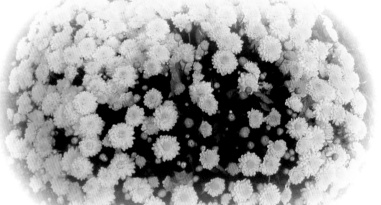

87 If you bought "clean" straw bales for your Halloween decorating, do not throw them away. Clean straw bales—those with no weed seeds—can be stored in a dry spot over the winter. When reseeding your lawn in the spring, the straw makes a great cover. It provides warmth and aids in moisture retention until the grass seeds germinate. The straw hastens the germination process and ensures that your seeds remain in place until roots can anchor the plants firmly to the earth.

When that fall chill arrives and you are forced indoors, you don't have to stop gardening. There are lots of fun projects to extend the season. One of the best is to create a beautiful and functional topiary. Pick up a pot of rosemary from your local garden center or dig one from your garden. Choose a nice pot, put a topiary ring (you can form your own from a coat hanger) in place, plant your rosemary, and fill with soil. Wind the branches around the ring, securing them with green florist's tape. Make sure you don't twist them too tightly or you risk damaging the branch. Secure the tips at the top with twist-ties. Now trim the shoots into a nice shape. You will need to trim as the topiary grows to maintain the shape you want. Save these trimmings; you can dry them for flavoring in the cold winter months. There, you did it; won't your friends be impressed?

Holiday
Plant Tips

89 Taking care of poinsettias is not hard once you learn a few rules. Rule #1 is easy: Never let a poinsettia wilt! They are not forgiving. Rule #2: Always keep poinsettias in a warm room—60 degrees Fahrenheit or more—and avoid cold drafts at all costs. Remember, the poinsettia is a tropical plant. Rule #3: Never let a poinsettia sit in water. Those pretty foil pot covers hold water and will kill a poinsettia in no time. Keep the soil slightly dry, water thoroughly when needed, and then let the soil go slightly dry before watering again. Follow these rules and you'll have a happy holiday!

90 Ever wonder why that poinsettia from the year before didn't turn red in time for Christmas? Well, poinsettias are photo-periodic—they are sensitive to the amount of light they see during a day. To make them turn red on time, make sure they don't see any light after 5:00 p.m. from October 1 through the end of November. They need lots of sun during the day, but they cannot see any light after it's dark outside your house. This is where the idea of putting poinsettias in the closet (or under a black plastic bag) comes from. An unused guest room works just as well, as long as it's heated. If you follow the correct procedure, you should see the leaves change color starting around the third week in October. Keep the dark treatment going until the leaves have completely changed color.

91 Ever wonder why a poinsettia that you just purchased in a store looks wilted when you get it home, even though the soil is moist? When purchasing poinsettias or other greenhouse holiday plants, make sure you have sufficiently warmed your car for transport home. Prolonged exposure to freezing outdoor or car temperatures will almost assuredly cause leaf damage. The exposure doesn't have to last very long, either, so remember to warm that car and ask for a plant sleeve or bag.

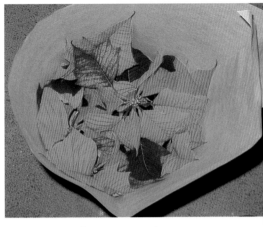

92 How do you get Grandma's old Christmas cactus to bloom again? Holiday cactus (Schlumbergera spp.) can be forced to bloom at any time of year, but it's easiest in the fall. Place the cactus in a cool window (it has to be sunny, though) and let the soil go dry between waterings. Watch carefully for tiny buds around October 1. After sighting buds, make sure the soil stays evenly moist at all times. Fertilize at least once after the buds have formed. In about a month you'll have spectacular flowers.

93 Nothing says Christmas for some people like the elegant amaryllis. Starting an amaryllis from a bulb is easy. Choose a large, firm bulb and a tall pot that is an inch or two bigger in

diameter than the bulb itself. Place the bulb in the soil so that ¼ inch of it remains exposed above the top of the soil. Water thoroughly and place the pot in a warm spot, preferably 70 degrees Fahrenheit or more. Let the soil get dry to the touch before watering again. Once the leaves and flower stalk have emerged and the bud has swollen, keep the soil moist so that the amaryllis won't wilt; wilting shortens the flower's life. Cover the soil with decorative sheet moss, the finishing touch on the perfect Christmas flower.

94 It's easy to rebloom your amaryllis. When it's still blooming, keep the soil moist but not soggy. Once it has finished flowering, cut the stalk at the base—but not the leaves—and continue watering until mid-summer. Now move the pot to a cool, dry, dark spot. Forget about it until late October or early November. Cut off any remaining leaves at this point and place the pot in a sunny, warm location. Start watering as before, and in about six weeks you'll have blooms again.

Narcissus (paper white) is a bulb that is easy to force indoors for holiday and winter enjoyment. Almost any container will do—paper whites are not fussy. Fill the pot ¾ full of good soil and bury the bulbs, leaving ¼ inch exposed, just as with amaryllis (see tip #93). If you fill the entire pot with bulbs, make sure they are touching each other for a spectacular display. Don't worry if the paper whites push themselves out of the soil as their roots develop; just push them back down.

Placing a layer of small, colored stones on top will help hold them in—and it's quite decorative, too. Water well and watch out, because paper whites grow fast and will produce flowers in about three or four weeks. Try storing some extra bulbs in the refrigerator and planting a few pots every couple of weeks. You'll have flowers all winter.

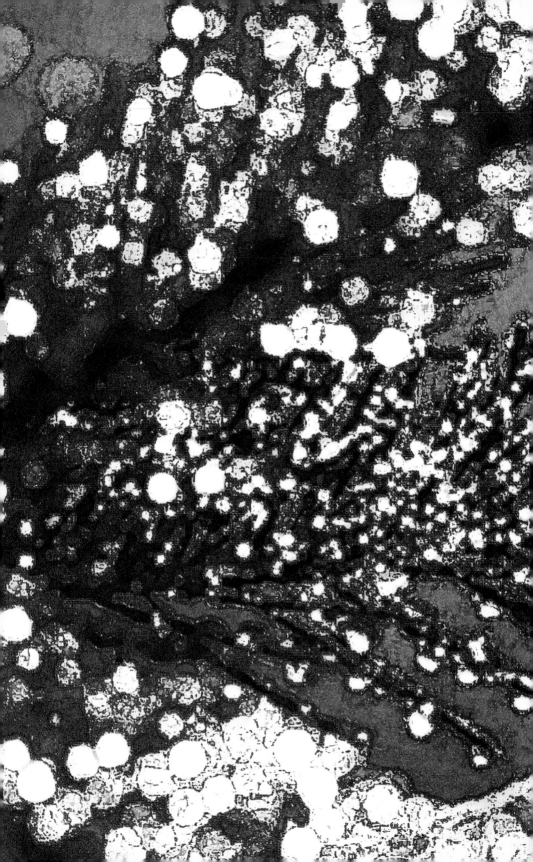

Christmas Trees

and Holiday Greens

96 There are several surefire methods for picking the perfect Christmas tree. Freshness test #1: Grasp the end of a branch firmly between your thumb and index finger and pull toward you. If no needles pull off in your hand, the tree is fresh. If more than four needles come off, look for another tree. Freshness test #2: Bend the end of a branch back sharply onto itself. Look for the branch end to snap back sharply, not bend pliably.

97 Always carry a tarp or blanket for tree wrapping and protection when transporting your live (balled and burlapped or containerized) or cut tree in a pickup truck, or when tying a cut tree to the car roof. Prolonged exposure to a cold wind (a car traveling at 40 miles an hour will generate such a wind) will substantially dry out any tree, decreasing the freshness and lasting power of a cut tree, or the survivability of a live one.

98 If you're planning to purchase a live Christmas tree in northern climates, dig the hole for its planting well before the holidays, when the ground is still unfrozen. Keep the soil you remove from the hole in a wheelbarrow and cover it or store it in the shed or garage where it won't freeze.

99 After bringing your cut tree home, immediately cut at least ½ inch from the base with a sharp saw and put the tree in a bucket of warm water while waiting to set it  up in its final display location. This will remove the gum callus on the bottom of the tree and enable more efficient water uptake, extending freshness. An aspirin in the water will also aid in liquid uptake.

 100 When moving an evergreen into the house as a living Christmas tree, do so in stages. An abrupt transition from subfreezing outdoor temperatures to 70-plus degrees Fahrenheit will cause plant shock. Instead, move the tree into a moderate temperature environment such as a garage for a few days, to lessen the shock. You should do the same on the way out of the house when it's time to plant the tree in the yard.

Most garland or roping has been cut and strung well in advance of the holidays. To extend its freshness, soak it in a tub or basin of warm water for at least an hour, then let it drain. Towel dry before stringing it either outdoors or indoors. This, and periodic misting, will greatly extend its decorative life span.

Index

Numerals in bold indicate photograph.

unusual containers, 51, **51**
watering, 48, **48**
Cow manure, 30
Crocus, 25

D
Daffodils, 25
Deadheading, 73–75, **74-75**
annuals, 75, **75**
Deer, protecting bulbs/shrubs
from, 25, **25,** 54
Delphiniums, 18
Dicentra (bleeding hearts), 16
Diseases. *See also specific diseases*
of African violets, 54, **54**
and debris, 9, **9**
of houseplants, and
watering, 37, 42
of roses, 31, **31**, 54, **54**
Drainage
for perennials, 16
testing for, 5, **5**

E
Electrical lines, buried, 3, **3**
Evergreens
choosing leader of, 10, **10**
and light, 70, **70**

F
Fall, 77–81
cleaning debris in, 9, **9**
indoor projects for, 81, **81**
planting in, 78, **78,** 80, **80**
Fertilizing
analysis of, 59, **59**
annuals in containers, 47
bulbs, 24, **24**
houseplants, 43, **43**

roses, 31, **31**
slow-release, 59, **59**
trees and shrubs, 9
Fine Gardening (magazine), 51,
51
Floribunda roses, 28
Flowers. *See also specific flowers*
bulbs, 21–25
deadheading, 74–75
holiday plants, 83–87
perennials, 13–19
roses, 27–33
Fungicide, homemade, 54
Fungus gnats, 58, **58**

G
Garland, 93, **93**
Grandiflora roses, 28
Gypsum, 30

H
"Hardiness Zone," 16, **16,** 19
"Heat Zone," 18, **18**
Holiday cactus *(Schlumbergera
spp.)*, 85, **85**
Holiday plants, 83–87
amaryllis, **86,** 86–87
holiday cactus, 85, **85**
narcissus (paper white), 87, **87**
poinsettias, **84,** 84–85, **85**
Horticulture (magazine), 51, **51**
Houseplants, 35–43
best care of, 41, **41**
cleaning, 41, **41**, 58, **58**
fertilizing, 43, **43**
insects on, 40, **40**, 55, **55, 56,**
56, 58, **58**
location for, 36, **36**
misting, 42, **42**